There Are No

Totemless

"Africans"

2095*

TOTEMS TOTEMS, HUTUPO IZIBONGO
GENESIS 49.. ALL EGYPTIAN/AFRICAN WILDFLIFE

Chapters...

Conclusion:

It Is not Hotep, But Hutupo!

Dedicated To My One

Creator, *Now Known by Thousands of names Who allowed me to be born in an Awesome Bantu Race through a phenomenal Mlambo/Myambo/Dziya/Siziba/ Hungwe/Hove/ Romwe/ Mazibukho~ Sithole/Gondho/Nyoni totemic tribes.*

To my wonderful wife and family, I say you top the marks.

To our Race I say this is our Time.

*To the spiritual family of friends and great co-workers @ **KhamitHEthics** guys it's time we rock the boat harder!*

Turning back No-more!

Last But Not Least...To all the countless Honesty Scholars Whose Works have enlightened millions Thank You. I see far because it is from your works that my ears hear, my eyes see and my spirit is divinised.

Stay blessed We have been Enriched.

Introduction.

There is not even one Black Person or anyone of Afrikan parentage who does not have Totems!

This is a fact.

 To others it will be indeed a staggering realisation.

SINCE Ancient Tribes.

From very ancient tribes to today many *Indigenous* folks are still deeply connected. Besides our modern names, most of us still carry other *non-official* parallel natural identities. Traditionally connected with Nature. For example, I am a Mlambo... meaning my ancestral and natural identity or ...Totem... is *water, rain, river or marine life*. Three of my great ancestors were popular Rainmakers. The last one to perform this feat, Madhochi Gadhlukahlu died in 1975 still a popular Rainmaker.

Our ancestors intuitively knew we were only one infinitesimal part of the total. Now, many think humans are the greatest and most important part. Still, we are only a negligible, small speck like a grain of dust on the seashore. A dispensable minute feature of the measureless cosmos? Who knows? Look at the Sun, matter and *the earth*. Yet we are part of nature, a child of Mother Earth.

Conceivably a conscious part of *Spaceless* **Spirit or Energy**. The ancients knew something of great profundity.

They revered with almost divine respect and awe: Nature. The shear waste and abuse of food producing soils, water and minerals in our so-called advanced civilization is proof of our simpleton frame of mind. A shocking parade of stupidity. It is amazing really that we have professors in this world today! Let us laugh at "us" with one hand over our own mouths!

Ancestral FOOD

Our ancestors killed only enough of what they ate. Used the skins, hooves and horns from what they had killed and eaten. They did not waste life, nor disrespect *spirit/consciousness* connected to the beast just slaughtered. In all, they honoured and thanked some hoary nameless *force* for providing life, nourishment, and comfort. In earlier days such recognition imbued them with a relationship that attached them to all. They esteemed visible and invisible entities, the power of the animal spirits and other natural systems. In religious ecstasy they danced wearing skins, masks, mimicking in singing praise, and prayers to specific animals. Food brought almost a gratifying state of mind.

Dancing and laughter springing up like flowers they painted animal pictographs on walls, their dwellings, caves, even their graves. Thus, asked they the Spirit In them for guidance. So that the consciousness of the animal that had been consumed would be invoked to bless not curse.

The spirit of the animal killed will thus be tamed! For in killing a deathly energy would descend on society filling it with negative energy. Causing a predatory sphere within Society. The goodness and grace of mother Nature was a "necessary ill" *SIMILAR TO actions in the toilet!* We honoured the spirit of our prey. Such acts allowed us to remain linked to these animals or trees as our guides. As we kept an observant eye on them, we learned how to interpret climatic signs in the heavens and around us. Therefore, the true connecting frequency of harmony and balance would be retained! Hatching and nurturing by neutralizing the death vibe.

This released power of the dying victim offered us vital lessons, in life, and passage even in death. It reminded us that all animals were our kith and kin. Hence, Nature had created dependence within this connectedness like a newly born kid that must suck to survive. Meat was consecrated first then enjoyed as food! You do not besmirch your mothers' nipples when you are grown up do you?

Tattoo or Totem!

Thus, even though animals were like our brothers and cousins their life sustained us. TODAY this has been verified by so-called Human Genome Studies. Humans share almost 98% Genes with gorillas! Most importantly, is the so-called scientific emphasis put by the "wise" in our civilization? In which we now have managed to shorten our life span. Filled it with all manner of diseases like cancers yet *"wisely persist"* in disrupting our DNA with Gmo foods.

The GREATEST danger today, is the
silent subconscious war of Totems by promoting
Tattoos. We know that no Afrikan who walks on
earth today is Totemless.

What is Your totem?
If you have no totem what does that mean?
Are totems important?
Where did Totems come from?
Can we adopt a totem?
Yes, without totems You're drifting.
You are disconnected from your ancestors.
Your bloodline is dead! We are coerced and
tricked to pierce our bodies. To construct
meaningless funny tattoos, which have no
Historical, spiritual as well as natural genetic
links with those animals with a dynamic ancestral
vibration?

These tattoos are a hiatus to the flow of our
actual power from our ancestors as well as within
in the animal kingdom or natural sphere.

The blood coursing in us knows this… but the
Brain has been programmed to shuttle these
connections from our conscious awareness. Is it
not time to ask; *what is my totem?* THEN move on
to emblazon a mental TATTOO in our
consciousness with our totemic symbol.

It's a Game of life. A mental war for your brain
and on culture.
In addition, it is all about POWER!
We share some vital messages in this Book.
Enjoy the journey.
Priest Teacher Rabbi
LMDumizulu
All Black people have Totems.

Meditate on the 33rd negative confession of Ma'at

I Will Not Commit Treason Against My Ancestors.

Indeed, It Matters Much.

You need your "totems". You must acknowledge them daily.

Not only for those who are encouraged to want to know their totems, it is worse for the masses in Afrika who know theirs *passively*. The "control masters" would forever cherish our indifference to totems.

What do you do about it? Yes, you know your totem is *Lion, Zebra, Water, Snake etc....* then what?

Does it Matter?

Most of us we have been born in cultures and tradition where we have been divinely fortunate to have totemic identities. But we Know we have ONE totem.

Right

Wrong!

It will be a wonder and shock to learn that IT IS IMPOSSIBLE for anyone born of a female and male to have ONE totem! This is an unfortunate splodge in an otherwise holy Bantu tradition.

A Mental/Spiritual blind.

So how many totems should one acknowledge? Not ONE!

Therefore, it is important that instead of passively knowing our totems we must *activate* them.

How?

By hanging images or symbols of our totems in our homes, cars offices etc. instead of celebrities or politicians.

Yet to fully benefit we must engross our consciousness in daily totemic affirmation. This is done via *recited totemic poetry, praise songs or phraseology*. In Bantu it is called Zvidao...

Chapter 1

Totems not Totem!

If You are an Afrikan, of African or "Black Heritage", a Negro or Bantu you have totems inside and around you. The one choice you have is to activate or not activate them. To use them or not to use them. Totems come with the package of being born African or Black! From Your ancestry, mixed parentage or one drop as long as black blood flows you can never wash or wish Totems away.

Even if you convert to other religions or spiritualities totems remain in the background in your blood and around you. Hence surreptitiously or openly haunting you or blessing you if you are lucky. Whatever the current status eventually a day of reckoning will meet you.

What are your Totems?

Do you know them?

Have they been stimulated or not?

If you do not know your totems and at the same time you are black it is a signal that there is an unresolved Ancestral incidence in your history. This ignorance about what your totems are is a confirmation of that incident. It is manifesting in your ancestral profile and has an influence in your life and will always stick out in your progeny.

Colonisation and Enslavement.

We all Know that for more than 1318 years of Islamic hegemony on black people and 600 Years of Christian Black Slavery and African Colonisation "They" worked So Hard and mercilessly, shedding innocent blood changing names. Effectively delinking you from your totems! Millions were bludgeoned to death in attempts to expunge this type of memory. Varying subtle methods were and are still effectively in operation to decimate our names. The idea is to totally and precisely Erase Names. Which in all tactics destroys our knowledge about Totems? Sadly, this is the status quo for millions of Black people. The majority of which have acquiesced and now bow down to Islamic and Christian gods.

Identity Lost.

Obliteration of our names eventually leads to the obfuscation of our totems. You have read the Book Roots. You may have watched the Movie based on Alex Haley's family history. **Kunta Kinte** was battered into a new name. When we think we have no totems or that totems are useless or demonic we are open to a new identity. Once we lose our identity we become "a new creation". We are now a Christian, Muslim or Atheist no longer a real full Afrikan.

In that state we are disengaged from our rich past. We are spiritual slaves to the ancestors of those who have captured us physically or religiously via indoctrination or sheer force and torture.

As proceed in such devotion we will natural defend our status quo. In such reverence we breathe life and power into those saint's, teachers', traditions and prophets.

The sad reality is this, these were actually dead! Our obedience, belief and faith activated by our moral support, faith, prayers and fasting gives these images AUTHORITY. Our OWN Original and Tangible culture, traditions, rituals, diets, clothing, marriage formulae, family and behaviour remains passive, immobilized and inoperable.

We are dead to our own heritage by identity, though we are alive physically!

Many of us today carry European, Christian and Whitey Arabic names. Has it ever occurred to us to question in retrospect why there are no Europeans, Christians, other gentiles, Jews or Muslims rush to change their names to carry African names?

OUR Ancestors Formulated the Idea of a Creator Now called God by others.

WHY Do other Religions prevail over us?

Precisely, the short and accurate response is this, they observe the law of self-preservation. If we are thoughtful and in clear grasp of our identity we too will exercise these laws. The power to define and possess is thus with us. Real Power dwells in self-Identity. Identity works with words, nouns verbs etc.

If the name you have is actually your name then you carry natural rights. You have the Power to define and ownership. These go hand in hand. One is the hand the other glove. We need both. The environment is hostile. We are engaged in combat to survive.

Consequently, what you conquer you own. What you own you name or rename. You name your pet, you name your slave, your invention and whatever you own. It's the law of ownership. It is never the other way around. Whether your slaves "name or rename" you, it's worthless. During the Zimbabwe war of "liberation' we used to call the then Prime minister of Rhodesia Ian. D. Smith, *"mgodhoyi"*. It never changed anything…

He still exercised master ship over us.

He had to be defeated in war.

Unless we remove ourselves physically and mentally from being owned by others we are doomed. On the other hand, if we think we have liberated ourselves and emancipation has proclaimed or reparations using fiat money or fake freedoms we lose bigtime. The biggest liberator is True Identity. Totems are a huge aspect of that identity. Re-connecting and activating our Whole Being as Afrikans is done via **TOTEMS!**

Chapter 2

Once More What Is a Totem?

What is a Totem?

Is there any connection between totems and ancestors?

How many Ancestors should You Know?

Do You have a Family Tree?

If yes how far does it go?

Who Has taught You about God?

Your mother, father, grandparents, Books, Tv, Mosque, Church?

Christianity labelled African ancestors' pagan.

If You are or of Afrikan origins and you cannot count more than 10 ancestors on Your Paternal side and Your Maternal side YOU are LOST!

Without Ancestry YOU have NO Roots...

Without knowledge of your ancestry you have no Totems.

Definition of Totems...

The https://www.merriam-webster.com/dictionary/totem *defines totem as an object (such as an animal or plant) serving as the emblem of a family or clan and often as a reminder of its ancestry; also : a usually carved or painted representation of such an object. b : a family or clan identified by a common **totemic** object. 2: one that serves as an emblem or revered symbol.*

Digest the following interesting definition comprehensively.

Read it thoughtfully...

*"**Totemism** is a system of belief in which each human is thought to have a spiritual connection or a kinship with another physical being, such as an animal or plant, often called a "spirit-being" or "totem." The **totem** is thought to interact with a given kin group or an individual and to serve as their emblem or symbol. The term totem is derived from the Ojibwa word ototeman, meaning "one's brother-sister kin."*

The grammatical root, ote, signifies a blood relationship between brothers and sisters who have the same mother and who may not marry each other.

In English, the word 'totem' was introduced in 1791 by a British merchant and translator who gave it a false meaning in the belief that it designated the guardian spirit of an individual, who appeared in the form of an animal—an idea that the Ojibwa clans did indeed portray by their wearing of animal skins. It was reported at the end of the 18th century that the Ojibwa named their clans after those animals that live in the area in which they live and appear to be either friendly or fearful.

https://educalingo.com/en/dic-en/totemism"
{emphasis Mine}

One more scholar......Egyptologist Gerald Massey

Totemism, Tattoo and Fetishism as Forms of Sign Language.

Gerald Massey

"So ancient was Totemism in Egypt that the Totems of the human Mothers had become the signs of Goddesses, in whom the head of the beast was blended with the figure of the human female. The Totems of the human Mothers had attained the highest status as Totems of a Motherhood that was held to be divine, the Motherhood in Nature which was elemental in its origin. from Totemism, Tattoo and Fetishism as Forms of Sign Language…"

Bantus Carry Totems.

Bantu Afrikans' culture, kinship and tribal social structures uses totems. One's bloodline or a totem links them to an extended family on both sides of with parents. Thus, all children, uncles, aunts, nieces, nephews, brothers and sisters regard each other as closely related by blood.

"Igazi lami, Ndewe ropa rangu. My blood kinsman...."

Body parts like legs, heart etc are well known totemic organs. So too

many African wild animals like, lions, buffalo, elephants, leopard, hippos, birds, zebra, snakes and so....

Animals of the African Savanna (Grasslands),

Animals of the African rainforest,

Animals of the African deserts all these have been used as totemic.

But what is the big deal?

What does it save?

Billions follow another Route.

Millions of Black people follow Christianity, Islam and Judaism. Educated folks are steeped in Evolution, Atheism and Agnosticism These all teach black people that ancestral totems are demonic. That they are useless, thus there is no big deal.

Christianity on Animal Symbols and Ancestry.

Jesus is The Tribe of the Lion Of Judah…

Adam named animals… why?

Genesis 49…Prophecies?

Numbers 2; And the LORD spake unto Moses and unto Aaron, saying,

Every man of the children of Israel shall pitch by his own standard, with the ensign of their father's house: far off about the tabernacle of the congregation shall they pitch.

the lion, man, ox, and eagle.

Deuteronomy 33

The KJV's renderings "unicorn" or "unicorns" are examples where the KJV may not give the most accurate or precise rendering of the Hebrew. These renderings are found in the KJV nine times: Numbers 23:22, 24:8, Deuteronomy 33:17, Job 39:9, 10, Psalm 22:21, 29:6, 92:10, and Isaiah 34:7.

Ishmael Dube.

Does the Bible then acknowledge totems?

Christians are trained by Europeans to think of others answers away from totems

Jesus Himself indicated (Matthew 17:10-13 and Mark 9:11-13) that John the Baptist, by his actions, had fulfilled the prophecy by Malachi that Elijah would return.

Elijah would be **an ancestor** right. Notice that Elijah was a Powerful miracle working ancestor! In the Old Testament, the Torah Moses began chapter 5 with these words: *"This is the book of the generations of Adam. In the day when God created man, He made him in the likeness of God"* (Genesis 5:1). Then followers a list of dead people! These are chapters 4, 5, 10 and 11 in Genesis that enumerate **genealogies.** Why?

Why is the bible filled with these lists of ancestors? Has Christianity ever encouraged African followers to revivify they ancestral lists?

No!

Jesus is called the Lion of the Tribe of Judah. The phrase is found in the New Testament book of **Revelation 5:5**: Why? Why not simply God?

*"And one of the elders saith unto me, Weep not: behold, the **Lion of the tribe of Judah**, the Root of David, hath prevailed to open the book, and to loosen the seven seals thereof."*

This is widely regarded as a reference to **Jesus** by Christians. Why then are his followers and admires never called *Lions of the tribe of Judah too!* By the way even Satan the devil is also called a roaring lion! So, there is more to animal symbols and ancestry. Why such poetic statements are in the Bible is not clearly explained by pastors for Christians to know?

Is there proof that Judah the ancestor of Jesus was ever associated with a Lion? And why?

Christian theologians may not know the real truth or they are scared of identifying the real answer. The clue is the apparent connection between humans, animals and other natural phenomena.

Chapter 3

Totemic Chapters in The Bible

The tribal blessings found in the book of Genesis Chapter 49 and Deuteronomy 33 are all Totemic. Not mere poetic labels. Prophetic in a very abstruse dimension. They are tribal Totems. They were also adopted from Bantus who still use them today. Tribal TOTEMS are emblazoned on indigenous aboriginal peoples of the earth in AFRICA and all over the earth.

Christians & Jews Mis-Understand This Totemic Chapter!

And now to my Christian and Hebrew Israelites friends get out your Bibles and Torah and see some things that are going to astonish you.

Comments on many of our explorations on Critical Afro Identity Keys have been Dismissed without proof. Almost all Scholars say Genesis 49 which we call the Totemic chapter a prophecy.

Jacob's words reveal *"things to come"* to his descendants.

Is this True?

Yes... Totems which these peoples didn't have will now come to them! Adoption is one method of "*Totemisation*" to coin a new word! See more of this later in the **Chapter 5**; **the 7 steps of Totemic Identification**.

Many Christian and Jewish scholars teach that Genesis 49 is essentially a series of prophetic blessings that preordains the social structure and characteristics of members of the 12 tribes of Israel......

What!

The original ancestor...

These scholars expediently DISREGARD the historical import of this momentous Chapter.

Yakuv/Israel was in Egypt! An Afrikan dominated civilisation. There were pyramids and thousands of artefacts with dual features. *Gods!* Ancient Black Scholars formulated the concept of the Creator now named God. They also defined a human being as a **Muntu/ Bantu**. An animal body with a divine Spirit/Soul/MweYa/UmoYah!

The Sphinx... Hore-Makhuti is proof of that dual nature. Staring to the east a carved lion with an Afrikan Woman's head. Of course, damaged by those who invaded Egypt. A marvel that should never have escaped anybody! All the Animals pronounced in Genesis chapter 49 were already Bantu Kemetic Peoples! They had studied their attributes, had deciphered their Cosmic Nurture, Zodiacal calendar and accepted them as Earthly Totems. When did this happen?

It is obvious that the first ancestor had the totems of the Creator and mother Earth. The story of Atum, Adam in the Torah naming animals is borrowed from AFRikan sources where Black People from times immemorial in Afrika recorded In Egypt had Totems already in Existence!

The so-called gods and goddesses of ancient Egypt, deemed idolatrous or ancestors worship found in homes and shrines in Inner Afrika formulated the Bantu concept of The Creator. They All stand as clear proof of the ancientness of Totems.

The Netchers were already accepted as daily powers!

Amadlozi....
Shavi/Zvipunha/Midzimu/Masvikior/MHONDORO!

Netchers are composite artefacts. They represent the attributes of the Most High Unkulunkulu, Creator of our Ancestor.The black Thinkers formulated.

Ra. god of the sun, Ra was the first pharaoh of the world, back in the days when gods inhabited Egypt.
...

Geb and Nut. ... Guvhu/Earth Nut Nyute /Sky
Shu. ... Air
Osiris. ... Ausare
Isis. ...   Isusu(us)
Set. ... Shata
Nephthys. ... Nepfuta(fiery)
Horus.........Horesu (Sky Cloud Sky Power)

Why is it that you have been brought up to think and believe exactly the opposite of what YOUR Bible says? Dismissing Totems as Satanic Yet Yaakov adopted them for the 12 tribes?

A totem is an animal, plant, another natural object like rock, river or tree that is connected to a person ancestrally…

animal kingdom, with examples like the lion (nyamuzihwa), the zebra (tembo), the eland (mhofu), the bird (hungwe), the crocodile (ngwena), the monkey (soko), the snake (mheta) and a few from body parts such as the leg (gumbo) and the heart (moyo).

In Zimbabwe there are about 25 clearly distinguishable totem lines.

Therefore, when Jesus is Called of *the **Lion of the tribe of Judah*** in Rev 5: it is because his ancestor Judah in genesis 49 adopted the Sphinx Totem! He added 2 more the Vine and Donkey! *"Judah, your brothers shall praise you; Your hand shall be on the neck of your enemies; Your father's sons shall bow down to you. Judah is a lion's whelp; From the prey, my son, you have gone up.*

He couches, he lies down as a lion, And as a lion, who dares rouse him up? The sceptre shall not depart from Judah, Nor the ruler's staff from between his feet, Until Shiloh comes, And to him shall be the obedience of the peoples. He ties his foal to the vine, And his donkey's colt to the choice vine; He washes his garments in wine, And his robes in the blood of grapes. His eyes are dull from wine. And his teeth white from milk (Genesis 49:8-12).

It is judicious that we learn from the TRUE Source of Genesis 49?

What these verses say plainly point to that SOURCE. Currently practised by Bantus.

Here Are the totems adopted by Yakuv for his progeny he adopted them from Bantu totemic worldview.

Genesis 49-

Reuben/Rubveni (lost Birthright) and Zebulun- Totem: Water

Fish Eagle... Hungwe...Dziva, Mlambo Ngwenya, Mhlanga, Hove, Siziba, Mazibukho...Musikabantu Dynasty... Turtle, Crab, Gakanje...Munjakanja... Water animal totems are as vast with meaning as the sea itself. <u>Water is a powerful symbol</u> in itself. It's a sign of cleansing, freedom and mobility. Most significantly, water as a symbol is a universal expression of the unconscious. Bantu/Egyptic Source...hippo, crocodile, **Set, Ammut, Taweret. Attributes: Strength, protectiveness, justice, benevolence (female hippos), the household. Set was thought to have turned into a hippopotamus during his fight with Horus**

Simon and Levi~ Moyo Murozvi.. Lozi...Levi/Levites

"Moses", "Miriam", and "Aaron" are Egyptian names, but these are not the only Levites to have Egyptian names.

Take, for instance, "Hur", "Merari", "Mushi", "Hophni", "Pinhas" (there were two of them), also Egyptian names.

The Levites are a tribe that emerged at the time of Akhenaten. Levites were housed in the place called Mallawi (Mallevi - City of the Levites)'

In Egypt the Levites primarily lived in a place called Mallawi. Ma means Land and Lawi/Lewi are the Levites. Replace L with R You Have Rozvi. They build City States. Zimbabwe When the Buba Priests of the Lemba tribe in Southern Africa settled in Southern Africa they founded the Lands known as Malawi.

THE LEVITES WERE RECOGNIZED AS A RESPECTED EGYPTIAN PRIESTHOOD:

Gatsi Mtapa

Moyo Apis.. Ba Ka Langa.. Sun Disck..

Remember Exodus 32: **The Golden calf incident. In all its sense it demonstrates the issue of Totemic contention, as well as the Great Year vicissitudes brought about through Cosmic Totems! This is again a very powerful chapter on totems and the source of the Torah which is Ancient Afrikan Mysteries commonly called Egyptian Mysteries, Or Khemistry (Chem Mysteries)**

Power, masculinity, fertility, regeneration
The bull was one of the most important animal totems/gods in ancient Egypt. When an Apis bull died, it was embalmed and buried in great honour. From 1390 B.C. onwards, the Apis bull burial grounds were a huge and growing underground system of chambers called the Serapeum. The mothers of Apis bulls had their own cult and burial places.

Judah and gad

Judah is a lion as already shown.

Isaka was totemised as Dube/ Tshuma/ sheep.

In **Ancient Egypt it was the donkey totem.**

Ram Banebdjedet; Khnum

Attributes: Fertility, strength, birth

Khnum created men on his pottery wheel.

An illustration of the bas-relief from the Tomb of *Ti* from Sakkara. This shows donkeys trotting in droves under the cries and sticks of their drivers.

beats burden donkeys. Again, Ballaam Totem the talking donkey! <u>Numbers 22:21-39</u> and Jesus rode his Totem to before his death! Recall the donkey was one totem he was given! <u>John 12</u>

Tribe of Dan. Snake Vahosvi...

The snake totem has been used as the symbol of medicine for thousands of years all over the world. In America the health care system itself is in a melting process of renewal. Snakes symbolize restlessness and the desire to seek and explore.

Snake inspires one to shed old habits or renew them just as it sheds off layers. Thus, one gets to their real self by going deeper into their core. Sloughing off the facade being forces the access to your authentic self in its truest form. Snakes are sly deceptive cold blooded the definition of the animal in millions of humans who must train harder to tame this energy. Snakes often help us face our darkness without fear, as doing so leads us to our inner light.

In ancient Egypt all Pharaonic headgear had a snake.

Egypt_Snake_Mummy_Coffin

tribe of dan.

snake-cobra-fire-worship-prayer. Thoth serpent

Nyaminyami -Is the Mighty Kariba God. In West Afrika is ONyame.

Watch the following YouTube Videos...

https://www.youtube.com/watch?time_continue=18&v=h5jxp9DQ_dc

https://www.youtube.com/watch?v=_onQXUoqJqs

The Shona people in Zimbabwe have snake totems that include python, double headed snake and ndara. They are the Hosvi tribe.

The python is important especially for its medicinal purpose in healing. Its fat was used for healing the sick by the traditional healers. The killing of a python or even its appearance near the homestead signified trouble.

In west Afrika the Igbos and many other tribes revere the serpent!

Asher... Osiris/Awusari

Naphtali Gumbo/

Shava eland…..

Genesis-49-21-Naphtali-is-a-hind-let-loose-he-gives-beautiful-words

hind is female deer, a doe

Benjamin- Soko Benjamin Bahlemini a ravenous wolf.

Joseph Nyathi… buffalo/Unicorn Rhinoceros (Chipembere)

The Following Dynamisms are activated once Totemic Powers are livened …

- Fire energy
- Initiation & Wisdom
- Healing
- Kundalini energy
- Growth
- Change
- DNA
- Enlightenment

Hebrew is a derivative of Ancient Khamit Mysteries…

	Egyptian	Hebrew	English

Ah Mose/Amasi (milk)	Amos	Amos
khamwe	Khaim	
Si Amun	Simon / shimon	Simon
Maya	Maya	Maya
Mary / Merit / Meryamen /MhereYaAmen	Mary Miriam	Mary Merriam
Tahut / Thoth / Djuhute	Dawoud / Dafeed	David
Penhasy	Penhasy / Phineas	
Meryre/Marayiro	Merari	
Oserseph / Yu Zaph	Yousef / Yossi	Joseph
Ramose		Ramose/ Ramirez
Atum/Atema (black)	Adam	Adam
Kefa	Eve	Eve
Shoshen/Shoshona	Shoshanna	Susan
Seth / Seti	Seth	Seth / Satan
Amunhu	Amon	Amon
Mahera	Maher	
Neith	Asenath	
Hrwn / Haron / herr Haruna	Aaron	Aron
Krest / Krast		Christ
Meshesh		Messiah
Se KaRe	Zechariah	Zakareyia
Aton /Adana/Atana	Adon i	
Herum Atif	Hiram Abi(f)	
Un-joab-endjed	Joab	
Maakhare Mu-Tamhat	Maakhah Tamar	
Ausar / Osiris	Assir	
Hur / Heru / Horus	Hur	
Roy	Roy	Roy
Takha/Taka		Tasha
https://www.perankhgroup.com/moses.htm		
Islamic destruction of African Totems		

Does Islam Promote Afrikan Ancestry?

Does Islam teach Afrikan followers to keep reverencing their ancestors?

Has Afrika benefitted from Islam!

Is Islam an AFRikan religion?

Is it better than Christianity, Judaism or African Traditional Religion?

Is Islam the original faith of our ancestors?

Let us look at this with the seriousness it deserves!

First let us emphasise this... THERE WAS NO Middle East!

The middle is Northeast Afrika which The British renamed and allotted without Afrikas approval.

Whitey Arabs invaded Africa in large numbers from 749 CE. *

They settled in Alexandria, Egypt. They were mistakenly seen as African cousins and were welcomed as saviours from the oppressive rule of the Byzantium (Graeco-Roman domination.)

*

https://www.modernghana.com/news/249409/1/arabs-mortal-hatred-and-enslavement-of-the-black-r.html.

Through Historical events and around the second world war Europe renamed North Africa as middle East... East Of London! Read more here. https://www.washingtonpost.com/news/worldviews/wp/2016/05/19/the-modern-middle-east-is-actually-only-100-years-old/?noredirect=on&utm_term=.d2b728d962a3

Or watch Our video. https://www.youtube.com/watch?v=d_r5hhfskiM

Some Islamic scholars on Totems...

We quote from **John Alembillah Azumah's** Book; The Legacy of Arab-Islam in Africa, p. 141.

Ibraheem Sulaiman, a widely respected northern Nigerian-Muslim scholar/activist, describes indigenous customs as 'reprehensible and evil' and states elsewhere that: '**Indeed, Islam does not accept that people should have customs or traditions other than religious ones; for if Allah's way is a comprehensive way of life, what is there for custom and tradition.'**

S.S. Nyang writes approvingly about the '... **processes of Islamization' successes of Muslims in many areas of the West Sudan led to the gradual destruction of the traditional cults and the emasculation of the old aristocracy'.**

Ali Mazrui on his part views trends of reviving indigenous African culture **as 'a threat to Islam'** comparable to secularism, albeit a lesser threat.

Although in practice Islam has a mixed understanding on the idea of ancestors its core teaching is against totemism. Because Totems are ancestral they are understood by so called

"Monotheistic religions" as other gods. Yet these same religions revere prophets', have holy Sites, carry symbols and other artefacts which they would die for to protect!

Ancestor worship is the custom of venerating deceased ancestors who are considered still a part of the family and whose spirits are believed to have the power to intervene in the affairs of the living.

Is it wrong to worship ancestors?

YES, Ancestors are dead physically. But their ideas and memories (spirit energy) survives inside our memories and blood. Their flesh, blood and bones have gone back into earth matter. But their genes we carry. It is IMPOSSIBLE to do anything about that.

Can anyone really worship a dead person?

No!

Chapter 4

The First Ancestor.

From the Hoariest Epo[...]
That Ancestor created
directly by the Creator!

Selected conscious creatures and symbols that contributed in social differentiation the unity of clans.

- **-an aspect in specific clan modelling fused their energy after around central essential attributes of the chosen animal, like bravery, courage, speed and wisdom.**
- **-Ndebele izangelo/izibongo were derived from names of the ancestors, for power and deeds. Action!**
  For example, '*abakoKhumalo ngondlangamandla***'**
- **-addressing each other with praise names (chidawo).**
- **-totems serve in Afrikans are scientific, not superstitious.**

Australian Indigenous People Totems.

40

'Dreamtime' which is also called 'Dreaming' is an oral communication medium through which many ancient traditions is transmitted across generations.

Dreamtime has no beginning. For it goes far back to Earth's creation. It is associated with the moment ancestral beings voyaged all over the Earth taming the land, mapping the sky, implementing laws and seedling life. Although Dreamtime narratives differ from tribe to tribe the underlying theme revolves around totems, taboos, rules and rituals. There are similar to Bantu village life in conduct, relationships, rules and rituals.

Aboriginal Totems.

Totems

Indigenous People in Australia and the world over have same principles on totems with Bantu. These are definite beasts, birds, floral species. We look at the Australian Totemic worldview. The Australia River Is viewed as a Rainbow and serpent just like the Nyaminyami of the Kasambabesa River (Zambezi River) In Afrika. Traditionally, each Indigenous person obtains a totem from their parents. The parent's totems came via ancestral lineages. Totems at times are carved into stones carried along as talisman or fetishes by an individual so that s/he could be constantly connected to his/her ancestors, the land and his/her tribe.

Below is a table with an example of the power and use of Totems.

Just like everywhere the totemic system was a social organisation too. It delegated robust roles which fostered social cohesion via kinship within the tribe, in some ways similar to how family surnames and titles do in western society. Tribal law, taboos, and marriages were all aligned within this system, to avoid genetically close marriages. Some of these systems were very complicated.

(http://manfromsnowyrivermuseum.com.au/early-indigenous-inhabitants-of-the-upper-murray/)

Scholars point out that the biblical Elohim created a totemic man, the legendary Adam with the tail of an ape, a lion, or other zootype. But the elemental powers were represented: Sut by the hippopotamus; Sobekhe by the crocodile; Atum by the lion; Iu by the ass; Seb by the goose; Taht by the Ibis; Anup by the jackal; Kabhsenuf by the hawk, in whose likeness's totemic men. This first man was the Adam, who failed. He had no soul. No vitalizing sparks. Therefore, he had No fatherhood; the man who was only born of the group in communal marriage under the matriarchate lacked power to give life! But the ATUM was too Divine. Thus, the Mixing (hybridizing) occurred to Create the Original BLACK MAN the original Ba Ntu! MsikaBANTU! MsikaBantu MusikaBantu

The power of totemic Praise, dance and sound mimicking each totemic animals' behaviour links Our musical prowess with natural source.

In Southern Afrika via totems the Bakuenas of crocodile men and call it their father and their chief is the Great Man of the Crocodile. They would dance and choreography in deeds and thoughts patterns similar to the motion of Marine animals. So too the, Nyathis mimic the buffalo, the Ngara/Nkala the porcupine, and the Tshumas the men of the wild sheep, Sibandas the Lion Dance. Specialised totemic cults Built the Force Of Invincibility dominated all Black Peoples. The Loss and watering down became our demise. do with dance?

Totemism represents fusion, a state of non-differentiation that reflects in a very primitive way a manner of thought and feeling. It reflects aggregation and group unity based on similarity and sympathy. In other words, it stresses participation with the non-human world.

Totemism proper is practised essentially by hunter-gatherer peoples with their totems linking them to a non-empirical world that allows them to believe in the unity between them and their everyday world (Cooper, 1995).

Only minds completely crazed or fatally confused by the current Christomania and would suppose that the details of Totemism, which are as old at least as the Cult of Ptah in Memphis are Pagan. Some vital observations are needed here.

The royal regalia of ancient Black Rulers and sages demonstrated the development of therianthropic religion from theriomorphic. The totemic arrays of the Egyptian Pharaohs "...symbolises the fusion of tribes which led to the unification of the kingdom...

Other Totems.

Totemism characterize religious beliefs of many indigenous peoples. The **Sauk and Osage peoples of United States**, carry totems. The animal totems like Black Bear, the Wolf are adopted as animals for them and their desirable personalities used in praise. Scholars say the Ojibwa had tribal totemism which divided them into a number of clans called doodem, dodema, totema (we judge).

The Birhor tribe who dwell in the jungle region of the Deccan province in India also have totems. All Indigenous people on earth have these totems...

Chapter 5

Power of YOUR Totem.

Your Totem is an ancestral encryption. A spiritual switch. A special type of Operating software. A spiritual barcode. A spirit symbiological code. It represents a mystical or ritual bonding of unity within a tribal group. Amongst the Bantus totems play fundamental liturgical and libation roles in spirituality, religious and social cohesion. Powerful Identity tools. Cultural and educational tools. Totems must be the basis for any Afrikan integrational model, Unity, Pan-Africanism, Political, economic, legislative, military and Governance.

If You do not have Totems and you are Black then there is a History behind that. Find the causality of this loss. If you also have totems you have to galvanize them daily otherwise they are dead asleep.

It is important for every AFRikan to Know their totems.

A minimum of 2 totems is a prerequisite to actively stack YOUR part in critical rituals which mark the African Consciousness and cycle of life. If not, You are still going to Re-incarnate Until you get this right. Why should you activate your totems!

Why?

Because You are the Original Being.

Role Of Taboos.

As the Original humans we were the FIRST to interact with life frequencies in multiple dimensions when conscious. Trance of energies tame and wild. We resonated with spirits of vegetation and animals. Our ancestors therefore formulated Rules of engagement called. Call them Taboos.

The fundaments of YOUR Life are Bound in Great and quick Cycles within creation. Being a Muntu/Bantu, you are a spirit essence inside an animal body.

Your sociological energy can only be rediscovered regularly via the primordial Ancestral memory which was passed from his/her blood to you....

Yes, The Creator is the original giver. Our first ancestor the first recipient of that life Energy at the inception or origin Her/His creation. Therefore, there are behaviours that are to be avoided. These are Taboos.

Now

Let me cite from the article "Taboo" in the Encyclopedia Britannica by anthropologist Northcote W. Thomas,

"Properly speaking taboo includes only a) the sacred (or unclean) character of persons or things, b) the kind of prohibition which results from this character, and c) the sanctity (or uncleanliness) which results from a violation of the prohibition."

These include dietary observations like not eating your totem. Sexual behaviours like not marrying or having sexual relations with tribal members who share the same totem.

Other taboos are against-

Cannibalism. ...

Incest. ...

Abnormal sexual relationships. ...

Bestiality

Homicide. ...

Suicide. ...

Eating Cadavers. ...

Eating Carnivorous Animals. ...

Foods and drinks.

Totemism exposes our awareness that humans and animals share the same life frequency. Hus our living conditions and divine essence through that Energy crisscross seriously. Discord or harmony results from how we interact with Nature. Totems are the rungs up the ancestral ladder that eventually ushers the climber into the presence of the Creator of OUR Ancestors.

Over 100 plant and animal species are considered totems among the Batooro (*omuziro*), Banyoro and Baganda (*omuzilo*) tribes in Uganda, a similar number of species are considered totems among tribes in Congo (DRC) and the Central African **Republic, (CAR).**

For example, among the Igbos certain animals 'are' regarded as sacred and, therefore, not to be hunted or killed. Such animals are appreciated by the adherents of traditional religion. Any harm to them is a serious taboo, the violation of which is regarded as *nso-ala* (abomination).

Christians are known to have gone on and killed such animals...

Read ***Things Fall Apart By Chinua Achebe*** ... Okoli killed and ate a sacred python! Chinua Achebe also recorded the situation when Nwoye, Okonkwo's son, was converted. He hunted and locked up the royal python in his missionary box. That action of his worsened his already sour relationship with his father and the people of Umuofia.

What most early converts to Christians in Anambra area did was to kill the *eke Idemili* (the sacred python belonging to Idemili deity) *deliberately* and *use them as food*. Not only that, they killed and ate this totem animal, they put its head inside match boxes which when picked up and opened by the traditional religionists, they had to offer special sacrifices to cleanse themselves from the abomination because they had seen the head of *eke* (Royal python).

This brought the first physical conflict between the traditional religionists and the Christians in that part of Igbo nation.

Sacred mother hood.

According to Ancient Africans "creation" was mainly limited to the bringing forth life - the life of water, fish and fowl, animal, reptile, and other forms from the meskhen or creatory of earth, all these were and are sacred. Because they represented the womb of Apt the pregnant water-cow. This idea of birth from the womb is portrayed in Apt the first Great Mother **http://malikjabbarbooks.com/masseygenesis.html**

A **mother goddess** is a goddess who represents, or is a personification of nature, motherhood, fertility, creation, destruction or who embodies the bounty of the Earth. When equated with the Earth or the natural world, such goddesses are sometimes referred to as **Mother Earth** or as the **Earth Mother.**

Is TOTEMISM ANIMAL WORSHIP?

In The history of religious ideas, the belief that the earliest gods were animals or plants is prehistoric. It has been archetypal, resolute and adaptable. According to Egyptologist Gerald Massey one of the oldest accounts of such beliefs, McLennan's work had implications for the field of history of religion.

In the study *The Worship of Animals and Plants* (two parts, 1869–70) McLennan suggested a connection between social structures and primitive religions; and he coined the word "totemism" for the social function of primitive religion.

And YET we Know Now that such studies went deeper to delink all black people from ever using totems. Massey continues to suggest that **a totem whether a natural element, an animal or a plant was never meant to be an object of worship.**
We know through cultural practices and taboos that Totems were first a means of distinguishing one clan from another, a division, a vortex of energy, a god, a Netcher. That all energy is traceable all the way through one's genealogy to the Beginnings.
In effect it is a way of knowing one's ancestry and racial Origins.
Your motivation, drive, Power of Imagination and creativity Is Enhanced when your Your Totem is aroused through song and praise!
Praise poems (detembo) electrifies your confidence and self-esteem.
Solidifies Your inner sense of worth and identity.
Sharpens Your destiny!
Without Your totem within your self-esteem sphere all Praise go no deeper than the cerebral cortex. Become Ego Boosters. Pride builds up. They are in the Short-term memory. Therefore, not yours but artificial or ephemeral, transient and fleeting.

Why?

They have not passed on into your Ancestral memory Bank!

Your totem is the link line. The Software that will transmute all praise to real spiritual value.

HOW Then does A Totem link You with That Ancestral Vault?

How Can they be delinked, disengaged destroyed?

Only by sheer neglect and Disconnected memory.

Tem/Dema/Temo/Demo NETER= Creation Laws within Totems.

The crux of TOTEMISM is in recovering Ones identity. It is a living Afro Symbolic Language. Through it The Rich Deposit of Ancestral energy flowing across generations can be tapped. One must be aware of one's totemic "animal" attributes. Positive ones and negative ones. These have a powerful mental or spiritual influence. Sheer talent, hard work, luck, prosperity, health, happiness and other needs were traditionally known to be positively ACTIVATED or deactivated via YOUR TOTEM.

If Need Be ADOPT Totems TODAY!

Many will ask quite correctly how if they have no totems, can they rediscover or recover their Totems.

We shall summarise the 7 steps in the next chapter. These Can be followed to revive and reconnect with their totem.

Chapter 6

Find Your Totems....

If You do not Know your Totem

Follow these 7 Steps.

Step 1-Ask Your biological Parents, Grandparents, Relatives or tribal Neighbours.

If they don't know.

Go to step 2

Step 2-Find from Your Tribe or oral or heraldry about Your Ancestral Lineage.

If No again go to step 3

Step 3 ~Law of Familiarity…. Which tribe are you attracted to. Who do you look like? Engage in serious verification process: Employ

Spiritual Research.

(Induced Dreams; repeatable dream)

(Use the feathers of Ma'at)

(Employ Meditation or Yoga)

Step 4-External Help. Find Wise Priests Who by Casting lots can assist. Send your email request to:

E mail... lmdumizulu@gmail.com

Specify the exact results from steps 1-3,

5 ~Try DNA or Blood Tests. DNA-results are not 100% trustworthy.

Warning the accuracy from DNA tests are useful as a mere step to locate the geographic and tribal groups your genes came from. Thereafter you will have to verify using steps 2,3, and 7,

On DNA we are aware that the results maybe too general as to be personally meaningless or that they are just speculation from thin evidence.

Step 6-Adopting Totems...

Please Note ... This is what Jacob did in Genesis 49. His father Isaac had no totem, His grandfather and grandmother Abraham and Sarah respectively had no Totems. Thus, he adopted common Bantu Totems.

Adoption… involves selecting any desired animals, natural or body parts as preferred Totems. Once selected there is no correction! Stick to them.

Extended family then emerges. An ancestral bank with all taboos comes alive. BEHOLD YOU ARE HOME! Intricate kinship, with tribal parents, children, uncles, aunts, nieces, nephews, brothers and sisters, all regarding each other as closely related begin to form networks.

Lastly

Step 7-Pouring Libations.,

The origins of the ritual of libation are so ancient and so important that even our record in Kemet are obscure, lost in the mists of time, and therefore accounted for in legend and myth. The African practice is the pouring of alcohol or other drinks as offerings to ancestors and divinities." (Armah, 2006, p. 207).

You pour libation and ask your ancestors to REVEAL YOUR Totems.

"Whoever does not inform his children of his grandparents has destroyed his child, marred his descendants, and injured his offspring the day he dies. Whoever does not make use of his ancestry, has muddled his reason Whoever is unconcerned with his lineage, has lost his mind. Whoever neglects his origin, his stupidity has become critical Whoever is unaware of his ancestry his incompetence has become immense. Whoever is ignorant of his roots his intellect has vanished. Whoever does not know his place of origin, his honour has collapsed"– Timbuktu Scholar 14th Century.

Slaves and dogs are named by their masters. Free men name themselves– Richard B Moore

Pour libation for your father and mother who rest in the valley of the dead. God will witness your action and accept it. Do not forget to do this even when you are away from home. For as you do for your parents, your children will do for you also– Book of Ani (Khamit)

Here are powerful keywords on Libation. Some familiar Bantu words.

Kuteyah, Mudiro, Uakorhwa, ukukolwa,

Tools..Water, clean spring water, beer, wine,

General Libation method.

Select a natural gourd, a good quantity of beer, water, wine as libation liquid. Find a quiet place if it's a private libation. Make sure you can pour directly into the actual earth and drink the remainder. Time: is usually early morning…

Other uses of libation

It may also be deployed to issue curses upon wrongdoers.

The libationer(s): the one(s) who perform(s) the ritual, enter(s) into this undertaking in order to recognise and proclaim the existence and superiority of those higher powers;

From the earliest known times, libations are always poured as part of the rituals which mark the African cycle of life: **Naming** Ceremonies, **Initiation** Ceremonies, **Marriage Ceremonies** and Transition Ceremonies (funerals). Libation is also poured at other occasions, such as to mark the settlement of a dispute, before chopping down trees (individually or parts of a forest), at the

Enstoolment of Chiefs, at the many festivals in the African calendar

Totemic Benefits

Since Libation reconnects our lives in oneness with the Supreme One, with the divinities, with the ancestors, among themselves singly and collectively, and with the physical environment IF we have Totems or in search of Totems This step will always play a crucial role.

A particular libation may be part of an occasion specifically devoted to the Supreme Being, or to a particular divinity, or to an Ancestor, or even to a living leader, but every part of African society is usually acknowledged in the statement accompanying the pouring, including families, clans and the entire collective. both 'transgenerational and transcontinental'. (Asante and Abarry 1996, p.60).

Chapter 7

HOW Many Totems Can You Have?

The traditional Bantu persistent male dominating perception. It is merely an idea with no basis in practice and reality. A traditional and cultural misnomer. We actually have More than One Totem? Is this so?

Yes!

The base limit is ONLY 2.

How Is this so?

Natural genesis and archetypical origins Limit our Totems to 2.

Which ONES?

The biological father.... And Your biological mother!

This is obvious...

Following this clear fact, it is apparent that from this base 2 we have almost countless totems if we chart our family tree back to the Creator Of Our Ancestors!

However, of the basic two IF You SNUB ONE its corresponding to walking with one eye open or hearing with one ear or trying to walk with one leg!

If You Ignore Both its like walking Blind in this world.

ONE HAND CAN NOT Clap! Chara Chimwe hatchitswanyi inda...

(one finger cannot crush lice....)

Mudzimu wokwa amayi une Ngozi...

Here is an example ... when you get married... you pay the lobola ... BUT a special cow is given to the mother!

Mombe yehumayi!

Is It possible to activate Both?

Yes, that is the purpose of the 7 steps given above.

Proof of totem linkages all over Afrika...

The 15 Anlo Ewe Clans, Totems & Taboos... The 15 clans are Laƒe, Amlade, Adzovia, Bate, Like, Bamee, Tovi, Klevi, Ɣetsofe, Agave, Tsiame, Amɛ, Dzevi, Vifeme and Blu.

Adzvia Clan:

Totem: Adzɔvia, a small brown perch-like fish related to Tilapia Melanopleura (Akpa)

Taboos: Members of this clan are forbidden to eat their totem fish. They are also forbidden to use unprocessed sponge (kutsamado-gbedi). They must not use the following local trees as firewood: Aviatsi, Xe and Xetolia.

In Zimbabwe South Africa Mazibukho Mlambo-Hove Ntini Siziba

Some Tribes changed totems.

Yes, many tribes who lost wars end up being assimilated into the conqueror's tribe. In such occasions they would perform specific rituals.

Some totemic taboos are primitive. The answer is a clear Yes/No.

Totemism, or tribe-heraldry, was not founded on worship of animals, birds, reptiles, and insects but on the energy or character traits exhibited these animals. A lion is a hunter and king of the jungle. So, Lion totems tended to be great hunters' warriors and fighters…

Atheism Evolution and Agnosticism.

Some Black African Free Thinkers following the cue of their Master European Teachers have ditched their Totems and adopted Evolutionary Theory. This teaching Dries Out Your Spirit in False Education. Disconnects one from their ancestry. Suffice to add that many trillionaire earth ruling elites, royal families, prominent citizens, powerful institutions all have Totems!

Your African distinctiveness Is Wholly Empowered by Your Totemic Identity.

"Thy perfect soul, O Nefer-Uben- f triumphant. hath the power of speech" (Rit., ch. 149, 15). Egypt was home of the seventh advanced Afrikan civilization, the last of its kind in the history of mankind. It existed at its zenith in North Africa but its beginnings were in the interior of Africa.

The achievements of this civilization included astronomy, mathematics, medicine and surgery technology, religion, agriculture, that is, domesticates, within the vast complex of this the Pharaohs annually sent messengers into the Kongo to bring the Twa dancers why?

There many features which link today's Africans to ancient black Egyptians such as similarity between ancient Egyptian language and Sub-Saharan African languages and similarity of customs.

Bantu have the same origin as Bachwezi, in Egypt. The most singular event which led to the mass migration of the Bantu was the liquidation of the Egyptian kingdom and its incorporation into the Persian Empire in 525 BC when Cambyses the Persian king occupied Egypt and killed the native (hence black king of Egypt, Amasis). This marked the end of native rule in Egypt (except for a period of five years from 404 BC) as thereafter the earlier referred to succession of foreign rulers followed (Persians, Greeks, Romans, Turks etc).

Totems denote common link.

The Bachwezi of the monkey clan (Nkima in Luganda), Abazirankende (in Kinyarwanda) reached present-day Rwanda and neighbouring territories, they would easily identify with those of the same totem as relatives, having common ancestry. My clan the Abagesera traces its ancestry to Kagesera, Ruhinda and Kimenyi and comprises of the Abahutu, Abatutsi and Abatwa, who erroneously colonial writers portrayed as belonging to different races! Their common totem is the monkey. **Read More** from:

https://www.observer.ug/component/content/article/57-features/feature/17487-feature-separating-myth-from-truth-in-bachwezi-tale

The West African coastal region comprises groups of peoples in nations divided into groups of kin. Twelve totem kindreds twelve names "...are derived from animals, plants and other natural objects, just as in Australia." (Lang, 1955 (i); Bowditch, 1873). The totem clans include the buffalo, plantain, cornstalk, parrot, wild cat, red earth, dog and panther. The Incra clan of the Ghana Ashanti are a clan of ants, which reminds us of "...a race of Mymidons, believed to be descended from or otherwise connected with ants, in Ancient Greece." (Lang, 1955, vol 1).

Again, in Ghana the Horse-mackerel clan believe they are descended from a man and a mackerel.

In east Africa there are many accounts that "...tell of the descent of man wholly from a totem animal...", and "...no mating with a human is suggested." (Freund, 1964). For example, the Masai, Nilotic pastoralists from Kenya and Tanzania, who believed they are from dogs.

In the Sudan the Shilluk attest they "...owe their beginning to the sacred White Cow of the Nile...a typical totem myth of this kind." (Freund, 1964). The Shilluk are a Nilotic population of southern Sudan and neighbours of the Dinka and Nuer. Similarly, the East African Wanika are from the hyena, and another African ancestor is the hippopotamus. The Wanika live in the Coast Province, the Shimba hills and east plains of southern Kenya (Rattray, 1878; Murcock, 1959). For some Malagasy people in Madagascar they have a lemur as the totemic animal which is known as the Betsimisaraka or Aye-Aye.

In totemic terms the Bechuanas people, who live in South Africa, are divided into the Bakuenas of crocodile men and call it their father and their chief is the Great Man of the Crocodile. The Batlapis are the men of the fish, the Banarer are the men of the buffalo, the Banukas are the people of the porcupine, and the Bamararas the men of the wild vines.

The Batlapis are the men of the fish, the Banarer are the men of the buffalo, the Banukas are the people of the porcupine, and the Bamararas the men of the wild vines. It is apparent that for north America and Australia that these people lived in a society with a specialised totemic organisation whereas, for Africa and Asia "...totemism is subordinate to, or at all events in close or equal association with other elements..." (Gomme, 1908).

Animal Worship

Totemism which has been simplistically described as tribal heraldry was not in fact "...founded on the human worship of animals, birds, reptiles, and insects. Zootypology, in totemism as elsewhere, did not commence as zoolatry." (Massey, 1888), and further totemism does not imply any worship of animals on the part of primitive man.
Anthropomorphic religion was heralded by totemism with which it was imbued with its elements and it was anthropomorphism that undermined and weaken the concept of the immolation of the god in the form of a divine drink and sacred flour (Reinach, 1909).

- Totems Are One of the OLDEST Linkages to the First Ancestor

Thy link you to the Hoariest Epoch Ancestor created directly by the Creator!

We have seen that conscious creatures must have contributed in some way to the existence of the clan.

-an important aspect is that totems are specific energy modelling around an essential attribute of the chosen animal, particularly bravery, courage, speed and wisdom.

-In Ndebele izangelo/izibongo were derived from names of the ancestors, for power and deeds. Action based!
For example, '*abakoKhumalo ngondlangamandla*'

-addressing each other with praise names (chidawo)arouses those attributes and boost self-esteem. -totems in Afrikans are scientific, not superstitious.

Chapter 8

Critical Issues On Taboos and Totems.

Writer and Egyptologist Gerald Massey researched and wrote volumes on Totems. One powerful term he uses in zootype. Zootype is defined in the **dictionary** as; *a classification of several phyla or groups of animals together based on shared chromosomes.*

Zootypes became means and models of communicating with nature. "modes of representation". They were the earliest means of recording human history before there were written records. Besides the use of signs and symbols, myth and totemism was enacted by the ceremonial dance. This is why, suggested Massey, the Khamite deity Bes an Inner African Neter, was portrayed as dancing.

When the Zulus say that mankind came "out of a bed of reeds," the typology is that of the Egyptian hieroglyphics in which we find one reed stands for "A," the old, first one; another reed, " Su," is the sign for the child; and the reed denotes origin for Egypt itself.

(*http://www.hermetics.org/pdf/Gerald_Masseys_Lectures.pdf*)

Some totemic zootypes such as the serpent, crocodile, hippopotamus, lion, hawk, and other figures of the elemental forces who preceded the human image become primitive type of power. The characteristic behaviours of these animals would later be adapted and transformed into totemic impulses within tribes…

Tribal Purity and energy attract Taboos. Violations of which neutralises this on many levels. Therefore, Christianity and Islam train followers to think that they could dislocate with license, the sanctions of traditional. These overzealous converts ignore and hence violate taboos and abominations.

Massey continues to teach of the six souls that gives human life. He says the seventh is the perfect one.

The Most POWERFUL Noun ON EARTH;

The 7th Is OUR Human Ancestor, "*Thy perfect soul, O Nefer-Uben- f triumphant. hath the power of speech*" (Rit., ch. 149, 15).

Man is created twice over in the book of Genesis. The first Adam is formed in the image of the Elohim or elemental powers. The Elohim said, " *Let us make man in our image, after our likeness* " (Genesis ch. i. 26). **(Massey Gerald. Ancient Egypt The Light of the World pg 432)**

"In the second creation man is formed by Iahu-Elohim, who "breathed the breath of life into his nostrils and man became a living soul " (Genesis ch. ii. 7) These two as Egyptian are **Atum - Horus and Atum-Ra,** who are identical in nature with the first and second Horus - the soul in matter and in spirit. The first man was a failure. In a gnostic version man was formed, but could not stand erect, because the seven workmen, the Ali or Elohim, were unable to inspire him with an enduring soul. He writhed and wriggled like a worm upon the ground. Then the " power above" took pity on him, seeing the creature had been fashioned in his likeness, and shot forth a spark of life which enabled him to rise erect and live." (*Nat. Genesis*, vol. ii. p. 39.) The most powerful noun on earth is a word that defines an animal with a divine Spark.

We continue with our investigation on the most powerful noun on earth. It must above all else cut across time and define a human fully. Before we share that most powerful noun let us look at Judaism!

Rabbinic Confusion.

The man created by the Elohim, or Ali, was totemic man, like the legendary Adam with the tail of an ape, a lion, or other zootype. It was thus the elemental powers were represented: Sut by the hippopotamus; Sebek by the crocodile; Atum by the lion; Iu by the ass; Seb by the goose; Taht by the Ibis; Anup by the jackal; Kabhsenuf by the hawk, in whose likenesses totemic men were imaged.

This first man was the Adam, who failed and fell from lack of the vitalizing spark of the individual fatherhood; the man who was only born of the group in communal marriage under the matriarchate. These totemic forbears of man may also account for a Rabbinical tradition in which it is related that previous to the creation of Eve the man Adam entered into sexual intercourse with the animals. *Which is doubtless an ignorant misinterpretation of the totemic status of man and animals made by theologians who were ignorant of totemic sign-language.*

Some of the Rabbis asserted that the first man, Adam, was created in the Garden of Eden with a tail like that of an ourangutang. His tail was afterwards cut off to improve his appearance. The legend contains a fragment of the mythos which has been reduced to the status of Jewish märchen.

This may furnish another link betwixt the Hebrew Adam and the Egyptian Atum, as the fiery-spirited ape was a type of Atum, the solar god of the garden in Amenta. [Emphasis mine….]

(Massey Gerald Ancient Egypt: The Light of the World (12 volumes in 1) pg 432)

Well Please re-read that paragraph…It is quite something!

Bantu Oral Ancestral Teaching and Philosophy Reveals that YOUR Patriarchal Totem is Vital.

The Igbo society believes in character and has very strong belief in life after death. Mbiti (1970) posits that when a person dies, his soul or spirit wanders around the bush, until his relations perform the necessary and befitting burial rites.

Hence animistic concept and sense of awe and sacredness of forests certain animals and other natural phenomena among Afrikans. Our AFRikan ancestors called humans Bantu! Tis noun has so many meaning we will deal with a few. The human body is an animal body. Science today tells us that we share 98% of our DNA with Chimpanzees. Why are we so different in terms of socio- cultural, technological, Creative and political output? The answer is the Divine Spark. Thus, the Bantu is a cognate of the divine nature inspired via the Ba Soul in a the Ntu the animal body. This is the totemic signature. The one explanation that that ties all loose ends into one holding anchor of life.

In hieroglyphics the noun is thus.

The Ba is symbol of Totemic nature of the human. OUR ancestors knew that a human is a spirit in flesh, bones and blood. A traveller, a wayfarer

a sojourner, a drop of ocean water and that We are on earth to complete lessons. We life in eternal conscious or energy cycles. Our time now is to gain essential experience of *matter in this dimension the 3rd dimension*. We are in the kingdom of matter fleetingly. Subsequently, we must mark our time and never allow our Spirit (divine nature/divine spark) to be enamoured or magnetised by matter or materiality. Even so we must perform our duty, master our lessons with clear cut distinction punctuated with great works otherwise, we will come back to relearn. Re-incarnate. Yes, life is a serious business. We are Bantus for a reason!

All Present lifeless religions and their lightweight boring and uninspiring philosophies have hardly scratched off the thing paint work on the syllabus of our training. The lack the intellectual stamina to face the germane questions, on what is real meaning of life. They have not clearly told us what is man? (Human)

They have not taught followers on How to live life in blissful happiness, health and embrace death with pleasure in old age. The saddest of all is the deceptive belief that we shall go to heaven, and some to hell or that it makes no difference to man's mental stability whether he knows he is traveling a brief and stony path to death and oblivion, or whether he is on his way, through storm and sunshine, to an endless unfoldment of radiant life. OUR ancient ancestors gave us the answers. Its staring you in the face...

The word is BANTU the Philosophy is Maat Or Ubuntu Unhu. All is oiled by adopting and activating the attributes of your TOTEM. The antiquity of totemism is known from ancient African deities Hathor Ithole- Sithole-Nkomo! Anubis Anpwa- Dog/jackal Anobvisa removes danger... being formerly totemic.

The royal regalia of ancient Egyptians demonstrated the development of therianthropic religion from theriomorphic. The totemic arrays of the Egyptian Pharaohs "...symbolises the fusion of tribes which led to the unification of the kingdom...

Chapter 9

Cosmic Nurture of Totems

In Ancient ages without televisions, the web, cell phones, electric lights night time transformed the earth into a completely different reality.

It would be too dark, mildly hued or very bright with the moon glowing. In this scenario it needed no genius among our ancestors to realise how much they depended on the Sun. For light by day and for light by night indirectly via the moon and the numberless shimmering stars, if it was cloudless and clear. Therefore, many lifetimes invested heavily in mapping out, studying by observing, learning and looking, not into a small square screen and hitting buttons, but into the far horizon upwards in the heavens.

In doing this, they then realized specific cyclical patterns, familiar animal shapes formed by various clusters of stars. These shaped heavenly beasts were seasonally in motion accompanied by various other heavenly bodies. This led them to realize the subtle connections and obvious exhibition of direct and indirect correlation in behavioural synchronicities with humanity. Thus, the localized Totem now jumped into a cosmic plane.

What then is our cosmic totem?

Is it the same with our earthly one?

Do we know? What is the answer?

When were you born?

What date is your birthday?

The day you came out of mom's womb into this **WORLD** or the day of FUSION!
When the sperm and egg or sperms and eggs excitedly *(electrical excitation)* fused and BANG began the journey of Growth that became you. At The instant of fusing was the divine spark created or not. Does the soul jump in or latter?
Considered lightly Science and so-called common sense and popular
tradition dictates that our birthday is the day of our parturition.
Is this correct? Is this the day we were BORN? On the other hand, is it possible our flesh is not us! We were born before that. Our flesh is like a radio in which we can tune to any frequency and hopefully tune the vibe of our true home???? Done within specific cosmic alignments?
With the totem as our area code?

When then is our true birth

The **Power of the** Sun.

The Sun without doubt is the source of all life on this planet called Earth. Without its electromagnetic energy, life would never be here. Thus, the Sun is the true source of life sustaining energy on earth. The pool of still waters! Yet we need not have any belief to accept that the Sun is a source of all the energy we need now, not some eons ago, or in the world to come.

The Milky Way,

Is the galaxy, in which our solar system vibrates, it is a spiral galaxy. Spiralling just like our kinky hair. It has about three hundred billion stars. Most of these stars are visible to our naked eyes. Thus, the wise of old mapped these stars and gave them names. They are reputed to be far bigger than our own sun. Hence, they influence our own sun! There are over **fifty billion galaxies**.

Could our potential be hidden in our earthly then **cosmic totems. Are after sojourning on earth and pass all the test ready to** be allotted more duties of rulership or control Even the ownership and ruler ship of galaxies?

 What a thought!

 THIS IS TOO hot!

However, please ponder on this matter with an open mind...Is there a superior intelligence preparing us for such a stupendous role?

How small shall our ideas of life be if ever this is true and we be manipulated into tattoos and **ignore totems**!

Cosmic Totems.

The knowing that predates religion, modern science or astronomy involved far huge expanse we call the heavens. Within this, it is a clear point of our beginnings as a conscious and individual entity in this vast expanse of space. For this reason, our Totem in the Skies or Solar Birth Totems must be brought into alignment with our earthly ancestral Totem. Yes, our earthly Totems not Tattoos must be of necessity like our Grade 0 in our school system. Totems are Not to be ignored. Last but not least they are our life's natural initiation keys.

Personal Map

Our Totems form a pattern for us. A spiritual network. The energy, which has become us came via two humans. Feminine and Masculine energy. They also were from a set. Tracing and viewing the rungs leads to the Creator. But the human permutations are almost infinite. The connection and networks too huge to imagine. We can learn many things. *Our personality, attitudes, abilities and shortcomings.*

A solar totem then encompasses many other aspects. This demands real knowing. It borders on the horizonal edges…. i.e. the milk way and beyond. Detecting the "subtle" force sleeping within us is easier if we think of dreaming.
Our Ancient Ancestors realized that the River Nile is an exact mirroring of the Milk Way. The Bridge into the new vibration when we die.
These Totems in the skies should lead us into this beyond… the cosmic system. But they must be connected during our lives by their earthly partner totems. From seasonal relationships to animal instincts we clan in groups. Just like the Astrological groups.

This totemic map in found etched in a calendar of reference in Afrika. At a place called Dendera. It is shown below.

Power!

Dendera
Earth Cosmo Livewire

TOTEMIC MAP

TOTEMIC LIKAGES

No Specific date of birth but a general period of starting this life.......

Within such a nurture we will be linked to many who may not be of our own race, creed, political system or whatever small narrow division imposed over us... *the limitless energy*...... but sharing the same forces with our intent!

We are closely linked *to **EVERYTHING***.

In Conclusion We Say

the real meaning of HOTEP—Is not Hotep...

You may have to watch this video…

https://www.youtube.com/watch?v=gYNhhFY5eUs&t=76s

Who taught us to say hotep?

Is it the right word?

In what context is this correct.

Could we know?

Yes, there are thousands of words we have been given all out of contexts and content. It is time to reveal the original meaning.

We all must learn and accept that European Egyptology agreed to use "a" and "e" between consonantal hieroglyphic words! Thus, the letters **HTP** would be hotep yet the context gives us the sacred word **Hutupo**.

Shown below is the hieroglyphic symbol representing hotep. Hutupo…Hutupo is Totem! The earth is connected in us. We have our Totems. We greet each other using them once we do that we arouse the energies of our ancestors flowing in our blood. We are energised. Therefore, the term Hotep as understood today is completely devoid of the totality of the AFRikan Ancestry and lacks the original Soul Vibration.

EACH Their Own.

Thank You for walking this far.

Priest Teacher Rabbi

LMDumizulu

KhamitHEthics

Any Questions...Email:
lmdumizulu@gmail.com

Visit Us on
~http://www.lifespiritofamenkhem.com

http://www.whealthiinc.com

Printed in Great Britain
by Amazon

38240881R00047